The Thanksgiving Turkey Pardon, the Death of Teddy's Bear, and the Sovereign Exception of Guantánamo

The Thanksgiving Turkey Pardon, the Death of Teddy's Bear, and the Sovereign Exception of Guantánamo

Magnus Fiskesjö

PRICKLY PARADIGM PRESS
CHICAGO

Prickly Paradigm Press, LLC
5629 South University Avenue
Chicago, Il 60637

www.prickly-paradigm.com

ISBN: 0-9728196-1-4
LCCN: 2003111000

Printed in the United States of America on acid-free
paper.

Introduction:
Secrets Hidden in Plain Daylight

The annual presidential pardoning of the Thanksgiving turkey in Washington is a full-feathered ritual. At its core, however, it consists simply of a brief public ceremony in which the US President extends mercy to a lone bird, namely, one big fluffy turkey that would otherwise have ended up on the Thanksgiving dinner table.

But this annually recurring event in reality is pregnant with deep and terrible significance. It holds the inner secrets of sovereign power, insofar as those secrets remain hidden in the archaic rituals in which sovereign power is constituted, recreated and perpetuated even in our so-called modern states.

"We have never been modern," writes Bruno Latour. And yes, we must admit that the visions of speed, progress, automation, social engineering, and so forth have come to show themselves more often than not as pomp, much of which is, moreover, orchestrated by forces beyond our control.

But even as all of this has begun to disintegrate, it is still very much apparent that we cling to the belief that we are modern creatures. We still crave affirmation that by the high noon of our own "today," we will be standing tall, high up on the ladder of civilization, in total control. And we are always, so we want to believe, advancing, moving further away from a distant, "primitive" past.

This delirious high oftentimes clouds our perception so badly that we tend to dismiss even the most central of the archaic rituals of power as child's play or innocent games which don't really matter. We laugh at them as cute oddities that must have been left behind long ago. Not so.

Ritual Mercy for the President's Turkey

The Thanksgiving turkey pardon is a prime example of an act that is only seemingly innocuous but actually serves to shape our modern consciousness. Masquerading as a joke, it is really a symbolic pardoning act which, through public performance, establishes and manifests the sovereign's position at the helm of the state by highlighting, as an attribute of this position, his power to control matters of life and death. Alas, the etymological coincidence of the words "executive" and "execution."

This symbolic pardon granted to a turkey, giving it a continued lease on life, signals the very manner in which sovereignty thrives on the exception: that state of willed emergency where raw power roams free, no longer bound by the constraints or directions of any formal law or legislature, casting aside such constraints in favor of the arbitrary. In this zone of exception, the life-and-death issues at hand are decided on the say-so of the one man whose body natural assumes the position at the helm of the body politic.

And so, the timely message of the Thanksgiving Turkey Pardon is that it raises the old challenges of power and governance, and, by extension, questions about how we want our world to be governed. How are we to condition and constrain the inevitable, the delegation of executive power to a sovereign?

Let's begin to answer this by taking a closer look at the strange non-execution of Bird Number One, the Thanksgiving Turkey.

This curious, apparent non-event takes place just ahead of the uniquely American, kin-centered and nationalistic Thanksgiving feast, which is celebrated each year on the last Thursday of November. This patriotic holiday is a very big deal indeed. It is a nationwide homecoming celebration in which a total of 45 million turkeys perish, as their flesh is consumed in the course of the Thanksgiving dinner. This feast is said to be performed by about <u>ninety percent of all American</u> households, and the turkey is the *pièce de resistance*.

The ritual pardoning of one federal turkey by the nation's President kicks off the feasting. As the nation's leader says, "Before I feast on one of the 45 million turkeys who will make the ultimate sacrifice, let me give this one a permanent reprieve" (from the remarks at the 1999 turkey pardon by President Clinton).

The President himself is the high priest of the pardon. It takes place annually in the White House Rose Garden, where it has been performed since, at least, we believe, the late 1940s. Its origins remain obscure—and regarding this mysterious obscurity, I'll have more to say later on. The tradition is nevertheless firmly established, cherished, and so important by now that we are safe to assume no President would dare discontinue it.

The journey undertaken by these American "National Thanksgiving Turkeys" on their way to the center stage of the Rose Garden is as exotic as any piece of strange ethnographica out of Africa or the Amazon jungle. If the matter at hand was the preparation of some similarly sovereign foodstuff, such as, say, the rice grown at a secret location in Japan to be served up to the gods by the emperor himself in one of the imperial rituals there, then surely a great deal of prayers would be said along the trail of the chosen bird, and the location of the divine growth would be kept a secret.

In the ostensibly secular USA, however, the precise location of the presidential turkey hatchery is no secret. The origin of the bird is rotated amongst active members of the National Turkey Federation. It proudly donates and delivers two turkeys to the White House every year. The rotation within the Federation seems to be undertaken perhaps more for the sake of advertisement exposure than for any sort of investment of ritual significance in the hatchery. The Federation chairman assumes the duty of finding, selecting, and setting aside a turkey from a farm in his home state. Likewise, one of his sons will often be selected to serve as the turkey's handler-in-chief at the high moment of the ritual itself.

The chosen bird is typically born in late spring. For example, the 1997 turkey was born in May of that year, alongside 2,000 other turkey poults, at the Tar Heel Turkey Hatchery in Raeford, North Carolina. In September, as reported by CNN, ten candidates were selected for size, feathers, telegenic posture, and docile temperament, at the tender age of sixteen weeks. In October, another "primary" was carried out to produce four contenders. Each year, in the days leading up to the event itself, the "National Thanksgiving Turkey" must be picked out of its flock.

A "runner-up" will also always be selected. This bird is sometimes jokingly referred to as a "vice-presidential" bird, one that is kept waiting, "in an undisclosed location..."

The point is to have a back-up bird ready, in case something should happen to Bird Number One. But the real vice president, notably, has no part in the turkey pardoning ceremony. It is exclusively reserved for the current holder of the highest office of the land—the man whose person inhabits the body natural must fit the tailored costume of the body politic.

Let's continue to follow the birds on their way. Both of the selected turkeys are flown to the Hotel Washington, in Washington, DC, where all of the chosen turkeys have stayed for the last 30 years. They are accompanied on their journey and at the hotel by proud Federation officials and their family members. On the big day, the "National Thanksgiving Turkey," together with its mate, is escorted to the Rose Garden in order to receive its pardon. Mercy will be granted this bird from the otherwise certain fate of being eaten like all the millions of others.

The "vice-presidential" companion, too, will receive clemency. But not in public. Instead it is set aside and kept waiting in a van, as a backup—a precaution observed ever since President Ronald Reagan got into serious trouble with an obstinate turkey that disturbed the ritual by flapping its wings in his face in 1984.

The bird selected for the actual performance is placed on a podium in front of attending officials and an invited audience of schoolchildren. The American people either are or could be tuned in to the event, through TV or radio broadcasts. Alternatively, the nation can receive the happy news through local channels. The mass media follow up on the story either through on-site reporting, or by spinning the story out of the official White House press releases. All that official material makes for eerie reading, listening, and viewing. It is available on the White House home page in audio, video, and written formats. This is in addition to the annual presidential proclamation of the Thanksgiving holiday, equally official and formal, which precedes the pardoning. (The proclamation has its own history, stretching back to George Washington's days. Sadly it is not something we can pursue here.)

With the bird on the podium, the preparations are finished, and the setting is finally complete. In keeping with tradition, the President directly addresses a short speech to the turkey, to the mass media, and the cheering audience of children on hand for camera effect. This speech includes the official pardon extended to the bird. Usually this is done with willful light-heartedness, along with jokes or playful comments about the bird at hand. The bird might add its voice to the exchange, thus serving as the butt of another joke. Occasionally the President will also offer a few answers to journalists' questions about the current issues of the day. This continues for a few minutes, while the schoolchildren are invited over to pet the official turkey.

And so, despite the lengthy preparations, the Rose Garden ceremony is over in just a few minutes.

8

As soon as it is finished, the consequences of the supreme command of a presidential pardoning comes into play—which is, of course, always the proper way in which the sovereign overrides judiciary decisions, or the normal state of affairs.

Both of the birds are now done at the White House, and they are driven to a final, fixed destination. This is a so-called petting zoo, the Kidwell Farm at the Frying Pan Park in Herndon, Virginia. Here, the two birds are received in a rather obscure and seldom-watched local-level sub-ritual of induction, which is framed as their "enduring" a turkey "roast," replete with "presidential poultry humor" and the cheerful reciting of "Thanksgiving history." While the birds are showered with greetings and, simultaneously, mocked, the children who happen to be visiting on that day will hear the story of how these turkeys are different from the other animals at the petting zoo because they "belong to our President."

Only after this reception may the presidential and vice-presidential bird proceed to their shrine, which is known as the Turkey Barn. The birds are then, in proverbial fashion, said to live happily ever after. In reality, however, they are usually killed within a year and stand-in turkeys are supplied. This goes on year after year. The chosen birds are killed because they have been engineered and packed with hormones to the point that they are unfit for any other purpose than their own slaughter and consumption. They are fast-forward turkeys. Presidential turkey caretakers have explained that most succumb rather quickly to joint disease—their frail joints simply cannot bear the weight of their artificially enhanced bodies. The sturdiest survivors may live a little more than a year. But the birds are always finally put out of their growing misery. Then they are buried nearby in a presidential turkey cemetery—the ritualistic significance of which remains to be explored. (May the archaeologists of the future excavate it!)

The task of these national turkeys, until they are out of sight, is to symbolically make way for the millions that will die (or which have already been killed and sold deep-frozen). Below I will discuss how this works as a first-fruit sacrifice. In this and in several other ways, the fate of the pardoned turkey actually coincides with the fate of the original "Teddy" bear, to which we shall presently turn. (As we shall see, Teddy was publicly "pardoned," but also suffered death sooner than we might have expected.)

Equally significant, and similar to the case of poor Teddy the bear, it is precisely at the point when these avian specimens are enjoying their moment in the spotlight that they are temporarily dressed up with a human name. In this manner—which is akin to the treatment of every pet, of course—the Thanksgiving turkey at hand is embraced and given the dignity of a symbolic subjectivity. The empathic President Clinton, for his part, used names like "Jerry" and "Harry" for the Thanksgiving turkeys that he pardoned. The latter name, "Harry," was in itself a presidential memorial, chosen in memory of Harry Truman who is described as the initiator of the turkey pardon tradition (but more on this below).

Moreover, Clinton claimed to have discovered different "personalities" in the eight turkeys that he pardoned during his two terms as President. That may well be: <u>Birds are people, too...</u> **?**

More insidiously, the fact that the turkeys are deployed as vehicles of human affairs—the manner in which they are used to address what are really concerns of human and not avian politics—is further underlined by the way they are humanized through the joking remarks setting them up for this game, all the while speaking to them directly. This business of unequal cohabitation with a pet animal at one's mercy is, of course, something rather widespread—not limited to the one-in-45-million turkey on the pardon stand—and it represents a sort of symbolic play that takes place within a loving and deep-seated Master-Slave psychological framework.

But this case of turkey play is clearly something much more. <u>It represents the most remarkably unequal and fleeting kind of acquaintance and joking relationship</u>. Consider, for example, how in 1999 President Clinton jokingly noted of the turkeys pardoned on his watch (eight turkeys in two four-year terms), that, "On occasion they're as independent as the rest of Americans." This limited-time-only and briefly conferred human status granted to the bird is an important indication of the notion of citizenship. This includes, as a core element, the acknowledged ability of an autonomous subject to make deliberate decisions for itself. In this sense the bird is really a ghostly figure of the Citizen. But at the hour of his reckoning, he is read his political rights. Oh, the humanized turkey, the token citizen, raised up on the pardoning pedestal as a signifier of the privileged bond your species enjoys with the sovereign!

This symbolic play takes many other turns. In November 2001, the sitting President, George W. Bush, named his first turkey "Liberty," using it to make a rather somber reference to the national emergency that had occurred only months before. The turkey of 2002, on the other hand, was pardoned by him under the name of "Katie." It was the first female bird ever used. Katie was named after the daughter of a chairman of the turkey farmers (the President apparently had not been told of this by the advisors who crafted the shift in policy emphasis, so he kept referring to the bird as "he" until late in the remarks). Traditionally, turkey toms (male turkeys) have always been chosen because they are bigger and so more of a statement, but of course tradition can be re-invented and often is. In the here and now, gender and diversity have been judged to matter more than size in the everyday political arena. And so the change.

To Eat or Not to Eat

The whole business of the President not eating the turkey, and more generally of political power-holders or officials casting themselves as arbiters in matters of life and death, brings to mind a wealth of other examples from human history. Including, of course, the political game of abstaining from the killing of living beings, and from devouring their flesh.

These issues are central to the quandary faced by all Buddhist *chakravartin*, or universal rulers: gaining and then wielding this-worldly power, but supremely abstaining from the evil of causing death. The paradigmatic King Asoka at first conquered by lethal force but then elected to take instead a pacifist position, propagating Buddhism. But how is the king to reconcile the acquisition and wielding of sovereign power with abstaining from war and killing, or with attempting to assume the position of one who offers clemency on a scale that might equal the compassion of the historical Buddha? For the Buddha, of course, killing was altogether abhorrent. The Buddha abstained both from the sacrifices of previous religious practices and from killing generally (he is, it is true, reported to have accepted meat as gifts). He abstained not just in one symbolically privileged case, but consistently. And so his approach is really a most radical formulation of a solution to these issues, a radical alternative. But this alternative remains hard to reconcile with the goal of achieving the power of an Asoka. Noble, yes, but it still seems that this

Buddhist approach remains far from compatible with the exigencies of kingship and, generally, those connected with executive political power.

Kings and other rulers are sometimes, for the sake of their own survival as sovereigns, <u>directly</u> <u>obliged to let the killing go on and suppress any</u> <u>expressions of compassion, whether occasional or</u> <u>consistent. One</u> example of this comes to us from ancient China before the advent of Buddhism. In the book of the philosopher Mencius, one king, an advisee, wants to substitute a goat where an ox should be used as the proscribed sacrificial victim—an offering to some ancestor god or otherwise honorable cause. The king takes pity on the ox that is to die, because he himself happens to see it, to see the sad look on its face. The king is overcome with commiseration.

But the king receives a stern reminder from his in-house philosopher (the equivalent of a spin-doctor): It would be a very bad idea to depart from the expected custom in this way. The uneducated masses would think that the king simply grudged the expense of an ox, as compared to that of a cheaper goat. And so, the political advisor famously tells the king that he must "stay out of the kitchen." That is, to stay away from the more brutal chapters of the handling of those lives that must necessarily be victimized in the interest of custom. The king, as king, inhabits the body politic, and therefore must reconcile himself with the killing of the ox whatever his personal preference. <u>Favor the body politic in your</u> <u>conduct, or abdicate the throne</u>! If necessary, "Stay out of the kitchen!" so that the show, which you are hosting, can go on.

In this connection, we can also notice the parallel that is offered by the rather more mundane games being played by contemporary politicians toying with vegetarianism. One example is the current Prime Minister of Sweden and the subtlety of his ambivalent comments hinting that he might, just might, really not like the idea of eating meat, and thus would be on the side of growing numbers of vegetarian and vegan voters. These activists, along with other animal-rights proponents, are vying with politicians for the privilege of defining issues of the day. One of the means available to them is redefining meat sold in stores as parts of "corpses." At times, vegetarians have seemed to be succeeding well in the ongoing battle for minds on this issue. Witness the continuing debates on the question of whether or not animals can feel pain equal to humans, radical vegan actions liberating farm animals, etc.

For a politician to oppose meat-eating—or at least letting it be known that he (or she) is considering sparing our four-legged and other friends—can thus prove a winning political strategy. It might help fine-tune one's image, using the technique of noncommittal hint-dropping by way of "code words," that some will say is very much in the "American style."

This manner of turning suddenly and subtly doubtful about eating the meat off corpses may well pay off in Sweden and other parts of Old Europe, as things stand today. But probably not so in America, the original home of the conveyor-belt approach to food processing, where people historically and generally have never been suspicious of the industrialization of slaughter or the outright engineering of animals into foodstuff.

Not-so paradoxically, this contrasts with the force of the image of the spared Thanksgiving turkey: Our jokes betray the realization that being roasted and eaten is not such a nice fate for any living being. Even the erstwhile dictator of Iraq was compared at times to a "turkey," in terms of the conditional possibility of being "let off," like the pardoned presidential bird offered a "way out of the oven."

Of course, the US has its own share of virulent vegetarian and vegan critics. Most particularly, one such view (Brenda Shoss, on animalsvoice.com) holds that the Thanksgiving feast on turkey meat is tantamount to feeding on the "carcass of [a] genetically mutilated and tortured bird," which has been "omitted from the Humane Slaughter Act," and bred "with growth hormones to concoct a breast-heavy mutation with swollen joints, crippled feet and heart disease." And PETA, the People for the Ethical Treatment of Animals, have recently recruited the music star Moby to make a free telephone recording which provides vegetarian alternatives to the Thanksgiving turkey centerpiece because "there is no proper way to kill and cook these beautiful birds."

Ultimately, though, in America, as indeed in many other times and places, such concerns for our two-winged and/or four-legged friends (cats, dogs, and horses excluded, of course), will invariably remain a minority view. Such compassion generally doesn't sell. The option of exercising it will seem less important for those in positions of official power than will the need to be seen as meat-suppliers—and the need to deliver forceful endorsements for the swinging of the executioner's axe, too. And so the ever greater contrast: the annual rite of clemency for the lucky bird let off the hook!

As a means of delving further into these matters—the sovereignly exceptional decisions over the life and death of human beings, and their relation to the constitution and grasp of power—we must dig even deeper into the specificities and the politics of the American Thanksgiving pardon. Because these turkeys stand for much more than their fleeting occupation of center stage might indicate.

The Work of Thanksgiving

In the pardoning ritual the giving-of-thanks is an example of the classic "first fruit" rituals and offerings described by anthropologists and other observers. The national feasting on the meat of tens of millions of turkeys is the main practical aim. But none of that can begin until one turkey waiting in the wings has been pardoned and restored to its source.

This is much like the classic salmon offerings of the native fishermen of the Northwest Coast: the ceremonial return of the fish (or of some part of it sent back down the river), the treatment of the first fish as a big chief who must be honored with a grand festival, or some other such act of symbolic voluntary submission before the powers of Nature.

In this way, both in the turkey pardon and in the honorific treatment of the first salmon of the season, the mass slaughter which everyone knows is to come is preemptively atoned for. This is done by way of the mode of symbolic substitution known as sacrifice. The gods, of course, most likely have no use for one simple, lousy fish or bird (they would be pretty lame gods if they did). But whether or not we believe in the existence of the gods, the point is rather that they might well accept that sign of submission or service which it constitutes. Their acceptance of this symbolic "gift to the gods" will come, hopefully, in the shape of even more such animals.

In the most general sense of giving up (rather than simply "giving"), the turkey pardon belongs with the sacrifices of the fish set free or, for that matter, the biblical lamb left to wander in the desert on terms set by the suprahuman. Admittedly, the turkey pardon may not measure up to quite the same lofty standard, since the turkeys have been tinkered with by us humans so mightily that they are manifestly unfit for a renewed lease on life.

Still, the singular, pardoned turkey specimen is similarly subsumed within a surge of gratitude that is mobilized and symbolically directed towards the higher powers or deities believed to be providing, from their end, the desired resource or state of affairs (such as: meat, dinner, Prosperity). In the modern, ostensibly secular USA, this in practice means the "Almighty God" invoked by public officials in need of divine sanction. The One On High ultimately guarantees there will be turkey on the table every Thanksgiving.

The chief's obligation to his community in this connection is to communicate with, and to please, the powers that be, on behalf of his people. This, it is believed, is his duty, necessary for the community so that it may be blessed with more of the same. The chief is defined as "the one" upon whom it falls to account for—or take the blame for—the actions of the entire community. He is "the one," much as the shaman in many traditions is the first to approach and the last to retire from encounters with the potentially deadly forces of Nature. By extension, and by exponential growth, this imaginary commander-in-chief also corresponds to the lonely sovereign of the famous expressions found in Classical Chinese self-referential imperial discourse, the Son of Heaven, a.k.a. "the one man."

Consider how the tradition of pardoning turkeys is regularly attributed to President Harry Truman in 1947. If so, it might perhaps have been initiated as a form of atonement after Truman became the first person to make use of his awesome position of power to drop atomic bombs. Towards the end of World War II the US successively gave up its earlier restraints against intentionally massacring large numbers of civilians. The awesome atomic bombs were, it is true, only the most flagrant example of this, but among the allied actions of war they outdid the firestorms unleashed in Tokyo, Dresden, and other cities.

We should consider such a technique of crafted atonement in light of Dennis Fleurdorge's theory of the "omnitemporality" of the President. Fleurdorge, as a student of French presidential rituals, observes that *le president* can be seen as located at the controls of a time machine, by means of which he masters past, present, and future. From this position, he can mastermind dealings with the terror of the capriciously unfolding events that make up real life, whether we like it or not. The sovereign makes sure that his people can redefine these events within a familiar, secure framework. By embedding them in commemorative rituals, anniversaries, cyclical highlights, and so on, he captures and tames any horror or emergency. This is one way to understand the customary, recurring President-led Thanksgiving ritual.

Facing and dealing with the capricious, exceptional nature of the event, and then returning to reassure everyone that normality has been restored, the sovereign (here, the President) will reaffirm the continuity of the state and both signal and realize its reconstitution in the face of horrible and tormenting upheavals and change. The element of soothing mercifulness that is enshrined in the Thanksgiving turkey pardon gives the go-ahead for the dinner gatherings of millions of families. It is reassuring and calming. Moreover all the people are in effect granted a presidential reprieve from the specific horrors of the day because, instead of the unpredictability of events, those in attendance can safely focus on the regularity of Thanksgiving. Take the day off and shut out the world because the "boys will be home" by Thanksgiving.

It is not unthinkable that the turkey pardon was introduced into the existing national ritual cycle after World War II to reassure the people that their imagined community was still, "after all," a good and godly one, just like before, despite the awful mass killings perpetrated on legions of defenseless civilians. If this interpretation turns out to be correct, the introduction would in addition make sense as a fitting renewal and expansion of earlier American Thanksgiving rhetoric. It would mirror the many Thanksgiving prayers from the post-conquest era in which European immigrants said thanks to their god for aiding them by exterminating the native Indians and thus clearing the land for themselves. (We'll come back to this.)

All of this may be true, but there is a small catch in the presumed link between these theses and the turkey pardon as we know it. The staff of the Truman Presidential Library in Missouri have been kind enough to inform me that although they, too, have often heard it stated, Truman did not begin the tradition. No. The records show that Truman, like Presidents before and after, annually received stately turkeys as gifts from the National Turkey Federation and from the Poultry and Egg National Board, or sometimes from newspapers and other well-wishers. But apparently he ate them all, never pardoning a single tom.

Well, well. Tracing a genealogy to a point of origin just may never work. Still, it is astonishing that we have to investigate such a basic issue as who first included the pardoning of a turkey in the duties of the President. Why should the origin of the tradition have been attributed to Truman in the first place? While we must set aside this issue for the time being, let's keep it in mind for some other day. Now, we'll go on to ponder the several other unresolved riddles of the turkey pardon.

We learn from this twist in the story not to be overly naïve or place too much trust in authority. Forgive me for pointing out, as an aside, that Mr. Clinton (or was it his administration's Thanksgiving scholar?) clearly was not forthcoming with the facts of the matter when he named the 1999 turkey "Harry" in memory of the ritual's founding hero.

So, all we know is that sometime after World War II, this public penitence became instituted as tradition. Before World War II, there seems to have been only one case of a presidentially-pardoned turkey. It carried some of the same symbolic force, but was rather more opportunistic and not a ritualistically institutionalized act like the one we know today. The turkey in question was pardoned by President Lincoln at the request of his son, Tad, who named it "Jack" and became its playmate in the lead up to its serving as a White House Thanksgiving meal. Jack never became a meal. Jack survived at least through the 1864 elections, as he broke into a line of soldiers voting in that election on the White House grounds. This prompted an exchange between Lincoln the elder and Lincoln the younger about Jack not yet having reached the age that would have entitled him the right to vote. Although he was a full-grown turkey, he was not allowed into the ranks of voters as a full member of (human) society.

Neither opportunism nor Lincoln's ability to make use of the turkey to teach his child the basics of voting procedures were, I think, the main grounds for the merciful exception granted in the celebrated case of "Jack." Instead, what was more important was probably the need Lincoln felt to demonstrate a spirit of "humble penitence for our national perverseness and disobedience," or, "the lamentable civil strife in which we are unavoidably engaged" during which he himself and his countrymen had stopped, on his instruction, for "a day of Thanksgiving and Praise to our beneficent Father who dwelleth in the Heavens," as Lincoln put it in his 1863 "Thanksgiving Proclamation."

"There is no honorable way to kill," was Lincoln's comment regarding the horrors of people killing people in the American Civil War. Lincoln was indeed winning the war but wasn't sure he would be able to win the peace. As it happens, the Thanksgiving holiday at that time was being zealously promoted by a devoted lobbyist, Sarah Josepha Hale. Obviously, Lincoln seized upon Thanksgiving's re-invention as a holiday to help collect the nation. And so Jack did not have to die.

Thanksgiving ensures the continuity of the American state. No wonder that at the turkey pardon ritual, Presidents will invariably speak of the fortunes of the nation, not of people in general, and they will highlight everything that the "we" of this particular nation are supposed to be grateful for.

To further emphasize who constitutes the "we" at hand, American Presidents invariably recycle the story of the Pilgrims and the so-called first Thanksgiving in 1621. It is to this story that I now turn.

24

The Displacement of Gratitude and the Struggle over the First Thanksgiving

The version currently in vogue of how Thanksgiving got going is, obviously, a nineteenth-century reconstruction. It is one that has been transformed into a powerful, taboo-ruled myth of the origins of the nation, the ominous "Us" which demands its "Them."

In the chosen story, the so-called Pilgrims (or the "Pilgrim Fathers") arrive from England across the Atlantic and land at Plymouth. At first they struggle, and almost die from famine, but from 1621 onwards they can celebrate harvests and Thanksgiving in a harmonious setting engaging happily with helpful natives who fix them up with fruits, corn, and turkeys.

The story is perpetuated not only in the presidential speeches at the annual ritual, but also in innumerable children's books, TV programs, and movies. Countless kindergarten and school teachers as well as parents have made sure that the version featuring pious seventeenth-century immigrant pioneers arriving in New England has become that which guides national consciousness.

Thanksgivingologists may debate whether or not roasted turkey really was part of the menu at the chosen feast of 1621. Even more interesting, however, is how the general outline of this crafting of history has been challenged by a host of new critics. They include such writers as James W. Loewen, with his biting and well-researched critique of American school textbooks, *Lies My Teacher Told Me*.

It turns out, for example, that the Pilgrim's Plymouth never was the empty place as painted in the national mythology, in honor of manifest destiny. Rather, it was the native town of Patuxet, the population of which had been earlier exterminated in European-derived epidemics (except for one person—the historical Squanto, first enslaved and taken across the Atlantic, then turned into a sort of mascot of the settler Pilgrims of the New Plymouth Colony. Recently, he has been reincarnated as a slightly more complex figure in *Squanto*, the movie).

Radical Indian activists in the USA have organized protest marches in Plymouth, begun in the 1970s by the late Wamsutta Frank B. James, a Wampanoag activist, descendant of the same people said to have attended the foundational 1621 Thanksgiving event along with their chief Ousamequin (or, more famously, Massasoit). Indeed, in the course of these latter-day iconoclastic protests, "Thanksgiving" has been re-baptized as a "Day of Mourning."

Alas, some even say it was never the gifts of friendly Indians that were gratefully celebrated by the "Pilgrims;" rather, it was the extermination of the natives and the Pilgrim's capture of the chief of one of the native tribes, whose head they cut off and mounted on a pole outside of their church. It was for this kind of progress that they gave thanks. They are said to have torn off the jaw from the dried-out skull, so that it would have to remain silent and have no chance of raising a haunted voice in the future to redefine this event for other purposes.

A process of self-questioning is presently unfolding in the United States regarding all of this. New scholars there take up and re-examine the old issues of the immigrant "fathers" and the competitive contemporary native Americans. David Murray, in his illuminating book, *Indian Giving*, recounts how the national myth makes the original hospitality of the Indians vanish as if by magic, and how the Pilgrims' gratitude is instead shifted and channeled to their god. This god is imagined as one that has sanctioned the new-found supremacy of their kind, and helped them regard the same Indians as greedy, dangerous sub-humans, i.e., that had better be exterminated.

This alternative history-writing generally lays more emphasis on the abandoned treaties, the forced death marches, and the terrible epidemics that decimated America and made way for European colonization, not least "New England." In sum, it lays out how the new polity was really formed through an "ethnic cleansing." King Philip's war—a war of ethnic cleansing if there ever was one—is the example most directly linked to the Thanksgiving story. The decapitation of King Philip, Massasoit's son, was only one generation removed from the early days of hopeful interaction and from those bright, reconstructed Thanksgiving feasts illustrated in today's children's books.

Granted, there are some children's books that try to contribute to the reconsideration of the roots of Thanksgiving as "we" know it. I have seen one (Edna Barth's 1975 book, *Turkeys, Pilgrims and Indian Corn*) which, in heroic fashion, exposes young readers to illustrations of how heads of the vanquished natives dangle from the settler's fortress walls, in the "custom of the day"—a scare tactic deployed to definitively subdue those who still wished to maintain their sovereignty and independence in seventeenth-century "New England." (Fig. 1)

[But even with all this criticism, and even with the attempts at re-writing history, in the orthodox understanding of the Thanksgiving meal and of the lore that surrounds it, the issue of the origin of the food and to whom grace should be directed remains largely concealed and semi-subconscious in the minds of those acting out the ritual.]Orthodoxy rules, and the thanks said for the copyright on the ingredients of the meal, despite their actual native origin, still goes to the acknowledged supreme deity and not to the former natives, their gods, or the American land.

This displacement of gratitude is also, in a strange fashion, still mirrored in the route traveled by the turkey itself. Originally a wild native American bird, specimens were brought to Europe from America by the earliest European explorers of the late-fifteenth century. No archaeologist has found turkey remains in a Norse or Viking site yet, but both Columbus and Cortez are believed to have carried turkeys on their return trips. And in the early 1500s domesticated turkeys were already being raised in several European countries, including England.

Figure 1. Colonial-style display of how to "kill the chicken to scare the monkeys." (see page 49 below) From Turkeys, Pilgrims and Indian Corn *by Edna Barth, illustrated by Ursula Arndt. Illustrations copyright © 1975 by Ursula Arndt. Reprinted by permission of Clarion Books, a division of Houghton Mifflin Company. All rights reserved.*

So it was that the "founding fathers" actually arrived not only quite some time after many others, but they came onto American shores not as empty-handed virgin children of their god but already armed with derivative, genetically engineered and value-added food products that belonged to them, and not to the Indians. The route taken by the turkey from forest to podium is astonishingly circuitous. The native American origin, and the subsequent return trip to and from Europe completed by the turkey before its final arrival at the Rose Garden and on the dinner table, is largely forgotten.

The turkey's story might have turned out quite differently. Just as the turkey's original route is sometimes forgotten, few have heard about the fierce battles fought over national avian symbolism. None other than Benjamin Franklin argued (unsuccessfully), in 1782, that the scavenger eagle was a bad choice for the National Bird which would figure on the Great Seal. The eagle has, as he pointed out, "a bad moral character" since he "does not get his living honestly." (Here, I am quoting Franklin from the pages of Allan Zullo's little gem of a book, *The President Who Pardoned a Turkey—And Other Wacky Tales of American History*.) It ought to have been the turkey, of course, that became the national bird. (Perhaps the pardon has been invented at least in part to make up for this historical mishap?)

The post-factum reconstruction of the travels of such founders similarly becomes apparent in the simmering struggles, between various towns beyond Plymouth, for the honor of having been the actual site of the Ur-Thanksgiving, that is, the site of the original receipt of the new land. In Florida, many school children have been taught that the "first Thanksgiving" took place in 1564, more than 50 years earlier than at Plymouth. Of course, people started giving thanks for the bounty of America 12,000 years ago, or more. But in this debate about when "we" first celebrated Thanksgiving, the other dates most often discussed seldom range further back than 1513. (Clinton joked postmodernistically about this "Florida recount" while issuing the turkey pardon of 2000.)

In any case, these various claims have generally been unsuccessful, because since the nineteenth century (and in particular since the orgiastic celebration of its 300th anniversary in 1920), the Plymouth version has come to serve a higher-order function. It is there, above all, to solidify the image of a benign melting pot, which must not be disturbed by the resurrection of such elements of history that are undesirable and therefore best forgotten. It is for this reason that Plymouth will almost certainly be reconfirmed, again and again, by Presidents and others, as the one foundational rock on which the national mythology will forever(?) rest.

And so, alas, despite the challenges, the standing of this Us-versus-Them-style national myth remains secure. This state of affairs almost certainly is due to the vital role that the myth has been assigned, in a fuzzy defence of the multi-ethnic American nation, something which requires a steady supply of feel-good mythologies.

It is due also to the peerless global power of the USA, which offers up a difficult challenge: to avoid being intoxicated by one's own patriotism, or overcome by the excessive conviction that one's might constitutes one's right. For in the USA, as well as in the case of every other grandstanding power in a similar fix, it's dangerous not least for public figures to appear as anything less than 110% "patriotic." And that's what one will risk if one expresses doubt about the mythological-foundational "Plymouth Rocks" on which the nation rests. One wonders if this was not why the US Senate, in the midst of the so-called Culture Wars in the 1990s, rejected a proposal (with a vote of 99 to 1) to create a more nuanced national standard for history writing in school books.

The dangers involved with questioning the foundational stories and their crucial functions are part and parcel of any explanation for why it should be so much harder for world power Number One to handle issues of collective guilt and history. Examples include the less-powerful state of Canada, the government of which recently apologized officially to the remaining native populations; and even multicultural Australia; or indeed the Pope's Church—full of skillful professionals, of course, when it comes to the timeliness of sensitive apologies and to the management of the channeled distribution of grace in this world.

But there is a deeper truth to this, one which perhaps will help explain not just the generality of the global rush to apologizing, but also the debates over impossibly guiltless politicians rushing to assume responsibility (and the right to apologize) for crimes none of even their most distant relatives ever committed, and other such strange new developments.

In the current debates over the world-wide flurry of We-are-sorry, few of the participants have observed that this storm of apologies isn't just due to globalization, which draws all of humanity into one big community, or to some more limited expansion of the frame of references within which wrongs ought to be righted—or compensated (many former natives or colonials have become global citizens) It is due, above all, to the fact that the lectern from which apologies, forgiveness, and pardons are issued, has come to seem more desirable in these times. This may sound like a pessimistic interpretation, but I think the basic reason for the flow of kind words is that the locus from which the pardon is issued is intimately associated with sovereignty, the source of the raw executive power that can undo and override the law. Their coordinates coincide, and would-be world sovereigns would all like to stand in that very spot, which appears like the shining throne of a magnanimous emperor in a globalized world. In the meantime, the real-world sovereigns pause, and say nothing.

In this era of global political restructuring, positions of power have to be reasserted, recaptured—or they may simply be up for grabs. Pardoning or apologizing, admitting an historical wrongdoing or forgiving historical offences: These are interdependent prerogatives structurally reserved for decision by the sovereign. Many are those who should like to sit on such a throne. At the same time, once on that throne, the tasks of the omnipotentate are never easy. Saying "Sorry" is hard. Pardoning is hard, too. And neither apologies nor thanks nor the pardon can be casually, or easily, offered by "us" to the dangerous enemies who must be lurking somewhere, even if they don't normally reveal themselves. And even more stressful than this is the fact that the real sovereign is the one who can least afford to show his cards. His own standing at the center of power, the place from which pardons emanate, depends on perpetuating the illusion that he holds the decisive card regardless of any "ought" or "should."

And it is precisely in this poker-game political context that the Thanksgiving turkey pardon provides a mirroring—yet revealing—window. Peeking through this window, we see at first a pretense of innocent "comic relief," then we notice that this is where the lonesome, naked sovereign is hiding: agonizing over his decisions, struggling not to show his cards and to make sure he stays out of the kitchen.

The Fate of the Original Teddy Bear (of Mississippi)

While the Thanksgiving turkey pardon, as an American ritual, is virtually unknown outside of the USA, there is another, more well-known figure that can help us recognize the plight of the sovereign. This is the world-famous teddy bear. The sanitized version of its original appearance on the scene is quite well-known. There is, however, a hidden core: the sovereign's pardon, which created "Teddy" in the first place, and its unspeakable aftermath.

Just like the turkey, our friend the teddy bear was also given a lease on life only to die another day, outside the range of the media spotlight. The death of Teddy the famous bear, just like that of the presidential birds, takes place away from the scrutiny of the symbol-laden play of a public pardoning ritual. The turkeys' deaths are meant to be unspoken, unreported, forgotten altogether. And indeed, as with the turkeys, the fate of the bear is ignored by the celebrating revelers, most of whom still believe (or, shall we say, "cling to the belief," in the manner in which we all cling to and keep hugging our teddy bears) that the original bear, the one that gave its name to our own, was probably left to wander off into the forest, back to its mama. Alas, that was not what really happened.

But let us first note that last year, in 2002, the cuddly teddy bear turned a hundred years old—cuddlier than ever. And, well, yes, we should celebrate that too, shouldn't we?

But the teddy bear stands for more than just a de-clawed original. Actually, its fate shares important features with that of the thoroughbred turkey's. Let's investigate. Let's "Dare to know."

Ur-"Teddy" is named after yet another American President, Theodore Roosevelt—a big game trophy hunter who traveled the world shooting animals around the turn of the twentieth century, an even more fervently "modern" time than our own. This was the era in which European and American big men took pride in expeditions and expedition photo-ops, featuring themselves lining up piles of slaughtered lions, leopards, elephants, buffalos, and so on, in the manner of ancient kings. Roosevelt himself is famous as a harbinger of the end of the game in Africa with his grand safari of 1909, an event that was most conspicuously unfolding alongside industrialization "at home." The astoundingly plentiful, teeming wildlife that roamed Africa would be no more, the first voices of protection for protection's sake were raised when it was realized that wildlife might be exterminated by "man's" industrious efforts.

Theodore Roosevelt's statue stands at the gates of the American Museum of Natural History, portraying him as a naturalist hero of the industrialist era, flanked by a Native American and an African, as if to highlight the breadth of the global conquests made by his own kind in the name of modern progress. This turn-of-the-century President, an icon of America, also hunted up and down the Rocky Mountains and other parts of the United States. For this he earned the scorn of Mark Twain and other

contemporaries, who suggested that he mostly had
his game dragged out of the wild, and even shot for
him. Roosevelt's virile pursuits, however, largely carried the polls of the day. The respect for him as
President-hunter had deep roots—deep down both in
old glories and in new science. It was also probably
related to the fact that Roosevelt had cast himself as
both an avid hunter and connoisseur of the wild,
something that hailed back to his youth, when he

*Figure 2. The Teddy bear and the President, according to Clifford
Berryman's famous cartoon "Drawing the Line in Mississippi." By
permission, Smithsonian Archives of American Art ©2003 Smithsonian
Institution.*

learned taxidermy, stuffing birds as trophy exhibits.
One of his areas of professed expertise was bears, and
he wrote at length both about their habits and the art
of hunting them. He was concerned both with their
killing and their long-term protection. *(army)*

During a hunting expedition in Mississippi, in
November 1902, game was scarce and it started to
look like the President was going to have to go home
without release of his executive (or, indeed, royal)
urges.

But his Mississippi hosts, wise as they were,
had anticipated such an awkward situation. So, they
caught a bear beforehand and tethered it to a tree.
They called on the President, who came, saw,
aimed—but then turned his gun away, supposedly
"out of compassion" for the already beaten and
bloody captured black bear, and also, obviously, to
stay true to his philosophy about the difference
between low and simple slaughter on the one hand,
and worthy, desirable sport on the other. (He was
reportedly also fed up with all the disturbances created by the newspapermen present in the hunting
camps.)

Some versions of the story say the tethered
bear was young, or a cub—others that it actually was
an old, lame bear that had been captured by an ex-
slave, who wanted to please the President. The latter
story seems more credible—and the shrinking of the
bear down to manageable toy size which took place
later was a different part of the story (see below). In
any case, the newspaper cartoons which followed
were composed on the basis of perceived presidential

pity for the animal, not the sportsmanship. Initially, they also seemed to highlight the President's free-thinking anti-segregationist race politics. (Thus "Roosevelt drawing the line in Mississippi," in the fabled cartoonist Clifford Berryman's formulation; Fig. 2.) Soon the bear was made a presidential campaign mascot, and, as everyone knows, the business idea of the teddy bear hatched out of the publicity.

Soon both the toy and the various versions of the teddy bear creation myth were mass produced throughout the world (such as in Germany). In the USA it became the first big hit of the Ideal Toy Company, founded in Brooklyn.

In England, King Edward VII, also a modern-style sportsman and huntsman, became enamored with a koala residing in the London Zoo. It became known as yet another imperial-style mascot and it too was reproduced as a toy, also under the name of Teddy. Whatever the original identity, Teddy's bear was a massive success, especially when it was shrunk to fit a new life as a favorite toy. Just like our latter-day cuddly toy dinosaurs, it comes softened and pre-tamed, and saved from itself: It has been freed from its annoying claws and teeth. And lo, ever since, the teddy bear has duly and obediently served as the soft bouncing trampoline of the modern subconscious.

"Teddy Bear patriarchy" is the heading of Donna Haraway's intriguing analysis of the diorama museumization of game animals in the American Museum of Natural History, in New York, which brought nature to the city for the edification of its denizens. And yes, the Roosevelt story and his role alongside the museum's creation above all evokes virility, trophy-taking, emblems of Man-the-Hunter, and the edifice of modern science. The hunting trophy competitions at the museum (in which Roosevelt served as a judge, for a while) have stuffed museums with such exhibited natural history as befits a patriarchal order, in this age of mechanical reproduction.

But the implications of the stuffed toy bear evidently run much deeper. Let's consider the story again, in light of the lessons taught by the Thanksgiving turkey. While every hunter with self-esteem would have done what Roosevelt did, note yet again that not just anyone could make the decision in this case. On this presidential occasion, the determination was up to, and only up to, the patriarch chief himself. Not just anyone could "give birth" to our very own Teddy bear.

Roosevelt's act of clemency aroused twofold and predictable admiration everywhere: both for his own person, and, in terms of the body politic, for his careful use of the presidential office and its privilege. On a deeper level, the case shows us the innermost constitution of sovereign power itself, which never appears more clearly than when it concerns decisions of life and death—and seldom clearer than in the case of Teddy.

Public decisions on life and death, that is. Like the case of the turkey, the public aspect is one which is most crucial. Here, too, it is connected with a rather gruesome cover-up.

When the well-known story of the origin of the teddy bear is retold (at the warm and fuzzy centennial celebration, for instance) the real and ultimate fate of the Mississippi black bear is most often ignored. When we look closer, we discover that the bear was really spared not its death—only its death at the hands of the President.

Roosevelt's decision not to shoot was based on his judgment that this was not a suitable or honorable kill for such a President-hunter. As he turned away, so the accounts say, he gave orders that the bear be killed "with a knife." Not by himself, that is, but by one of the Mississippians who had snared it for him. The President stays in the limelight, but "out of the kitchen."

We may recall that when the reporters are gone and the speech is over, the presidential turkey suffers a similar fate. Everything happens as if these terrible secrets, although readily available on the record, aren't part of the diet of public consumption. In the case of Teddy's bear's death, telling the truth probably would not help stuffed animal sales. In any case, this truth isn't advertised in toy stores, or in your mail order catalogue, or in the duty-free catalogs on airplanes, which often also sell such comforting bears—presumably not just for children, but a last resort when fear of flying becomes too gripping.

The death of the black bear was plainly announced in the newspaper reports of the day, but today it is not public knowledge. On one level, the sanitizing censorship which covers up much of the crude blood-letting that goes on in the fast-food processing industry, for example, makes sense. People in our time are more fearful of slaughter, even of the pig for Christmas ham, than they would have been in the bygone, more slow-paced era of a hundred years ago.

This is also, by the way, why it should not surprise us that the movie *The "Teddy" Bears*, released in 1907, features a Roosevelt character who brutally chases down the Three Bears of Goldilocks. For the full story of this once-happy bear family, I refer to Miriam Hansen's *Camera Obscura* article. Here I just want to seize upon the point that by slaughtering the parents of the Baby Bear, this Roosevelt reduces the original Three Bears to just the one little survivor. I want to suggest that this cinematic survivor's fate parallels the real story of Teddy's bear, and that this is an illustration of the chief's bond with the pardoned animal. The general pattern at work here is well-known: we kill off the more powerful grown-up bears, and capture the young for our zoos while the parents become trophies on our walls. In this case, however, the little bear seems readily identifiable as an alter ego of the sovereign—a symbol of the terrible power placed in his hands.

The comparison of "Teddy" the bear with the named presidential turkeys holds even though Teddy's christening was posthumous, and despite the fact that his fame is eternal, while the turkey's fame is bound up with the eternal rebirth of the species. They all "belong to the President," in the sense that they are named for him or by him, and a special relation is forged between them in the public eye. While all the little fluffy bears are Teddy's (Roosevelt's), by virtue of their mass production, all the pardoned

turkeys, too, carry the name given by the President—
even though each turkey is different.

The names of these tokens—especially, of
course, the presidential names of Harry, Teddy, and so
on—highlight the deep bond of the animal to its mas-
ter, in that the President has assumed the privilege of
deciding their particular fate and signals this by confer-
ring a presidential name upon them. (The deep significance of the fact that this concerns a living individual,
not just a picture or a figure of speech, will become
clear later—in relation to the Schmittian thesis that
"Sovereign is he who decides on the exception.")

This significance obtains even when the name
is ascribed casually or in jest. In fact, this pretense of
downgrading its significance is also significant. We
must remember that even when ascribed in such a
manner, the fate of the animal (life or death) is inextri-
cably and unavoidably dependent on the decision of its
"owner"—who precisely for this reason is the one in
the relationship who can afford to joke about it.
The rise in sales of stuffed bears coincided with an
explosion of teddy bear movie imagery, which in turn
fed on the toy stores churning out ever more reincar-
nations of the teddy bears. Suddenly, teddy bears were
in every child's room throughout the richer zones of
the world. And so the wild bear made way for the tame
bear and the stuffed bear, more malleable for our
human purposes. Granted, the practical reason for the
continuous recreation through breeding of the turkeys
remains that they shall be slaughtered and eaten. They
are not meant to live out the lives of their cousins, the
wild turkeys still found in America's woods. (As men-

tioned, the wild turkeys are already several genetic steps removed from those farm-raised that appear on our dinner tables).

Obviously the bears differ from such tame turkeys mainly as wild animals bred not by people, but directly by the gods. We people might like to think that this breeding happens in order to make those wild animals available for us to hunt, or for us to "cull"—but that is our own perception, contingent upon our history and presence in the world. Our furry friends probably see things differently—but their viewpoint is for the most part limited and reduced to the space of cartoon comics.

The original Teddy bear and the annually-pardoned Thanksgiving turkey are equally good to think, and equally good to use for the special purpose that we have revealed. On the most basic level, the clemency in both cases has really been granted by their public appropriation: ritual displays of power over particular lives and deaths through which they are transformed into the building blocks that help cement sovereign power.

Terrible as all of this might seem, let us now move on to an even more troubling cat-and-mouse game, yet other examples of the shadowy zone of pardons, this time in the purely human realm: First, to death row, and then on to the "War on Terror" camps at Guantánamo.

Death Row Clemency and Sovereign Power

The men and women on death row in US prisons, waiting to meet their fate, are entirely dependent on the mercy of either a governor of one of the sovereign states that constitute the US federal state, or, in the case of federal crimes, of the President himself.

The President is granted precisely such an open privilege in the American Constitution, and so are the governors, for crimes committed under the jurisdiction of their states. Any sentence can be commuted into a lesser one, and any crime pardoned altogether (with some variations in the legal system of particular states within the Union: in the state of Texas, for example, the sovereign's pardoning power is tempered, so that the state sovereign can only pardon those recommended to him by a board that he or she appoints).

It is not widely known that the distribution of the power of pardon for those condemned to death directly parallels, on the federal and state level, that of the pardon of the turkey. This logical possibility of the state-level Thanksgiving turkey pardon is actualized, for instance, in the gubernatorial pardon of the turkey belonging to the Governor of the state of Alabama. And there are some interesting, suggestive reasons for why this Southern turkey pardon should exist (and why no northern states seem to have their own—this awaits further investigation).

The American South is generally considered to have been slow to catch on with the Thanksgiving feasting tradition, long seen as a Yankee idea. But the lingering preoccupation with "state's rights" as opposed to the prerogatives of (Lincoln's) Union, has here found its natural expression in the independent adoption of the turkey pardon. The local governor along with other prominent men in dark suits and formal ties gather on the steps of that sovereign state's capitol, cracking jokes about the life or death and the temporary stay of execution of a bird which is donated, and treated, much in the same manner as that annually presented to the President. (If you think I must be kidding on this one, please take a look at a photo borrowed from the Alabama state governor's press office; read: Fig. 3.)

The climate of public opinion in the USA regarding state-sponsored judicial killing differs markedly from that of many other countries, probably not just because of cowboy history and other deeply engrained traditions, but also to some degree on account of the overwhelmingly successful run of the USA into high modernity and its ascendancy to a sort of actual world predominance since Roosevelt's times (indeed it has become a first world unto itself). This self-sufficient attitude goes some way toward explaining the recent outright refusal, last February, by the governor of Texas, to even recognize, let alone heed, an international court's direction to rescind the death sentence of two Mexicans. The governor's Missouri counterpart, on the other hand, recently suspended a death sentence on the direct appeal of the Pope—in person, in the city of St. Louis!) The self-assured position of the USA can account to some extent for the way the country has distanced itself from ongoing efforts to fashion strong international courts to deal with war crimes, and other high crimes against humanity.

In light of "domestic" opinion, it is very often not the decision to pardon but the decision to *refrain* from exercising the power to pardon that best furthers the political standing of the power-holder—an opposite tendency compared to that embodied in the animal rituals, where clemency carries the day.

One tragic example of the use of the non-use of the pardoning power (when the sovereign simply remains silent, thus permitting the execution), is the reported story of how Bill Clinton, then governor of another Southern state, Arkansas, chose to make himself unavailable to concerned members of the public when the moment of decision was drawing close for the execution of a mentally retarded black police-killer. The execution was locally popular, but probably unconstitutional. Unfortunately for the condemned man, the event was scheduled during the primary election campaigns in 1992. Here indeed we have a case of the executioner-in-chief "staying out of the kitchen." In concrete terms, this meant avoiding contact with lawyers and others aiming to press the point of the moral and legal conflict at hand.

Another example, but one which works in the opposite direction, is the recent conscientious objection to the very institution of the death penalty enacted by the governor of Illinois, George Ryan.

The personal decision of the governor to undo every
death sentence within his jurisdiction in his last hours
in office was based on the fact that the inherent flaws

*Figure 3. The turkey is pardoned—here, at the Alabama capitol, in
November 2002. By permission from the web pages of the press office of
the Governor of Alabama.*

and relative injustice (racial, etc.) in the use of the death penalty had been exposed more clearly in Illinois than in many other places. In the words of the governor, the administration of the death penalty was "wildly inaccurate, unjust, unable to separate the innocent from the guilty and, at times, very racist." By first vacating several sentences about to be carried out, one of them as late as forty-eight hours before the scheduled execution, and then also commuting the sentences of every death row prisoner in Illinois (altogether one hundred and fifty men and women), Governor Ryan "went into the kitchen" in a serious way and so made a different kind of history—sadly, only just before leaving office. "I no longer shall tinker with the machinery of death," the Governor said.

Governor Ryan also made clear that he thought his position was more important than any concern, real or populist, with obtaining revenge and retribution on the part of the wronged and the victimized. Friedrich Nietzsche, in his 1887 work *On the Genealogy of Morals*, insisted that the meaning(s) of punishment already had turned into a web of obscurity, beyond any (necessarily naïve) attempt at finding a simple definition. The philosopher nevertheless went on to excavate some might-have-been genealogies of the punishment of men by men and women by women: as outright revenge; as a grotesque "feast;" as prevention; for use as a declaration of war; and so on.

One of the prominent possibilities which Nietzsche listed was the effect achieved by punishment in instilling fear in those people entitled to see the punishment through, and carry it out, as well as in society in large. This preventive usage is found, in a slightly different form, in the Chinese proverb about "killing the chicken to scare the monkeys" (*sha ji jing hou*, a much-loved saying frequently used in China to refer to the realm of human punishments and political control of the populace, which itself is regularly compared to "a plate of fleeting grains of sand"). Somehow, it is suggested, the monkeys will get the point that it could have been them, that it could happen again, and therefore—at least for a while—they will hesitate before stealing another banana or troubling their would-be executioners in any other way.

In this sense, the meaning of punishment is unrelated to or even radically disassociated from the specific crime or the particular criminal and his victims where the punishment seems to represent an eye-for-an-eye correspondence. This happens even in countries that have done away with the death penalty and moved on to more sublime control regimes under "popular sovereignty."

[handwritten margin note: Sovereign power – Scapegoat]

And, significantly, notice that the dissolution in such countries of retributive or revenge-like justice, in favor of more modern-style social-management models, is not accompanied by the dissolution of the institution of pardon. Pardon, as the cancellation of punishment, lives on—not primarily as a tool of justice, but because it is an inescapable constituent of sovereign executive power. This was ignored by Kant, who envisioned no place for pardons in his famous constructs of ideal justice, where no one would act except as if the action would be worthy of becoming a universal law. Pardons would be out of place in the constellation of perfect justice amongst perfect people, where a king could pardon no one except those committing crimes directly against the king's own person. Pardons would, otherwise, constitute something of an affront to the law-abiding: an unfair usurpation of the right to punish transgressions against the law. Hegel for his part was famously opposed to depriving the subject-turned-criminal his right to receive his punishment. And the list goes on. This impossible absence of making room for the making of exceptions to the rule can be said to have persisted with, on the one hand, the general hope for universally valid rules guiding a rationalized social life (a hope bound to be shattered not by a God or by any new sovereign for that matter, but by the sheer force of historical events). And on the other hand, the philosopher's disgust for the thorough corruption and ugly commodification of pardons, both secular and religious, under pre-Enlightenment monarchies.

In this connection, it is also paradoxically fitting that the moral collapse of today's death penalty should have been revealed in Illinois. That state is home to a living relic straight out of the history of failed ideas of enlightened punishment: I refer, of course, to the surviving panopticon structures of early industrial-style prisons, which are still standing just a few miles from the city of Chicago. Otherwise such structures are nowadays mostly only theorized in books (most frequently in books written by Michel Foucault). They are partly still in use, including the "celebrated" central spying tower, but not in the manner that Bentham, their ideologue, originally intended them to function. Significantly, far from instituting Foucauldian ultra-anonymous surveillance, these structures are managed with a high degree of direct and personal guard-to-prisoner engagement. (At least this was the strong impression I got when visiting them: The cells have curtains, and the central surveillance tower seemed more like a guard's refuge.)

To dream of a world without pardons is to dream of a world without sovereign power. And some dream on: The constitutional prerogative for Presidents and governors to grant pardons to condemned men and women, in the manner of ancient kings, may indeed often be seen as hopelessly royalist, and potentially corrupting (because the king, or President, would favor his personal interests by abusing his power to pardon) even when considered as a "duty to be merciful." But none of this, by any means, gets even close to the core of the significance of the institution of the pardon.

To stop here would be simply to mystify the issue, as when one attorney in both the former Bush and Clinton administrations recently urged President George W. Bush to issue more pardons, "to send a sign that forgiveness and reconciliation are always within our reach" even within a system of courts and prisons which has become "harsh and less forgiving" (as put in a *New York Times* article, December 19, 2002). Well, yes, Pontius Pilate also used to pardon a condemned prisoner every year, letting the people choose him, so as to increase everyone's comfort (Matt. 27:15). For Bush to pardon some condemned persons would be laudable, of course, especially in view of the apparent retributive backlog and of the dismissal of the issue by presidential advisers (the sitting President granted no pardons or commutations at all in his first two years in office). Incredibly, this dismissal was made despite the long history of freeing condemned persons precisely on the occasion of Thanksgiving. The dismissal was, moreover, made in the style of the Thanksgiving turkey pardon, complete with joking references to the pardon of the bird, *as if this would be relevant* for the people on death row.

Still, monarchial forgiveness is but the flipside of monarchial corruption. All of this merely further clouds the true significance of the pardon in relation to the position of the executive sovereign—royal, non-royal, or post-royal. The same goes for other hopelessly utilitarian-style ideas that suggest pardons are for the concrete public interest. (These arguments are very often, I hasten to add, equally laudable. According to Francis Lieber's 1875 book *On Liberty*, citizens of Monterey, California, are reported to have gathered, in 1858, a great many signatures asking for the pardon of one José Anastasia, sentenced to die— because he was the only fiddler in town who knew how to play well enough for dancing parties.)

The core service of the pardon, even when its exercise is delegated to lesser officials, is not the benign benefit of all of society—however desirable it remains to find and secure forms for the dispensing of mercy. Rather, it is its role as a constitutive attribute of sovereignty. This is, I believe, the main lesson learned from the hall-of-mirrors carnivalesque rituals of the eternally-returning Thanksgiving turkey pardon, as well as from the fate of Teddy's mass-produced bear.

The power of pardon signals the location of sovereignty, which finds its expression in the decisions placed directly in the sovereign's hands: the decisions on wielding or resting the executioner's axe (whether in specific cases, as for fellow humans on death row, or animal by animal), or in the decision to make or avoid war, whether foreign or civil. And sovereign power finds its most obvious expression in—is always reconstituted in—every *concrete example* of every pardoned turkey or every exemplary teddy bear, as in the case of every death row captive, and, most important of all, in every decision on whether or not to trigger the suspension of normal order, as in that exceptional state of emergency known as "war."

Here (belatedly, you may be justified to think), we arrive at a point which demands that we confront the consequences of the pardon as exception, as identified in the famous dictum on sovereignty by Carl Schmitt in *Politische Theologie*. Schmitt preaches that sovereignty lies precisely in the power to decide on the state of exception—or, even more precisely, in the hands of that very *individual person* who has either seized or received that power for himself (*Souverän ist, wer über die Ausnahmestandezustand entscheidet*). Whether sovereign power is seized by usurpation, or democratically entrusted in some legitimate process, is irrelevant in this general formulation, which simply tells us what sovereignty is, by describing what the beast does.

Schmitt's definition boldly ignores the Nietzschean admonition that "only that which has no history can be defined," and many of the current writings on the topic of "sovereignty" fail to acknowledge just what is at stake here. Whatever else you may think of Schmitt (and this long after Schmitt's own preemptive tempering of his so-called "decisionism," and with due acknowledgment to the editors of *Telos*, who argue that the uses and abuses of Schmitt are more often than not guided by a *realpolitik* of the present which avoids the issues as well as Schmitt's ideas), surely both the assumption underlying Schmitt's dictum on sovereignty and its formulation still make sense. This is because among its many merits, it captured the crucial point that the exercise of executive power over the exception "still" necessarily lies in the hands of someone, a real person (or real persons) who makes the decisions.

This point is revealed by the general science of political theology. "The king has two bodies": the body natural, and the body politic. It is in the nature of things that the body politic must be inhabited by someone's body natural—and that the other constituents of that same body politic ignore the arrangement at their peril. This includes the body politic that is not of a monarchy, but of modern nations with presidents or popular-sovereignty states and other forms of democracy. The blood-drenched sovereign may have been clothed in other names, but has by no means disappeared in a vanishing act of the modern.

On the contrary. In the animistic rituals of the sovereign discussed above, it is up to a living person to play with and mock the animal's conditional citizenship or subjectivity. Without that person's presence, no play. Sovereignty similarly lies in the moment when the governor of a state is to sign or not to sign a request for clemency: a living hand must move the pen. In war, someone must personally say yes or no, so as to halt the army, or order it forward to clash with the enemy. This last point concerning war-making becomes yet more obvious with weapons of mass destruction, as manifested by the individual decision to punish the people of Hiroshima and Nagasaki, mentioned earlier. The problem of constraining the finger pushing such fearful buttons has been actualized again, after the dissolution of the former balance of terror between the two camps of nuclear sovereigns. Consider, as an example, the protracted deliberations regarding whose finger would be on the button of what became the sovereign state of the Ukraine, previously under the unified command of the Soviet Union.

It is, or should be, almost self-evident that there is a multiplicity of contending sovereigns in this galaxy of polities that is our present world, and that the precise scope and location of sovereignty and its jurisdiction is never final, but always fleeting. The possibility of more conflagrations like Iraq only serves to highlight the fundamental truth of the Schmittian thesis regarding the locus and basic features of sovereignty. In the case of Iraq, the decision on whether to let that country's sovereign become an oven-toasted turkey appeared to have been reserved, by unilateral declaration, by the sovereign of another nation, the United States. As if to reaffirm the Schmittian thesis on sovereignty, the President of the United States declared that neither the internal congressional questioning of the presidential prerogative to start war, nor the veto of the body representing the united nations of the world would matter. Of course, this stance represents a grave threat to the vision of a law-governed world. It also can be regarded as a case-book example of the perennial struggle over where executive power ends and how it can be subsumed under the law. The issue becomes whether such sovereign decisions as going to war can trump any law, by force of unilaterally perceived "emergency." It becomes, then, simply a continuation of one state's "foreign affairs"—which by name, by definition, and by the virtue of involving those nasty "others" still out there, remain the pet province of sovereigns.

The bond established in the relation of the sovereign and the exceptional, as during an emergency, real or imagined, is plainly evident here. The challenge for every society is how to organize the supervision of the release and exercise of such power. The challenge today is how a global society can achieve such an organization of itself. To forget this point would certainly be to abuse Schmitt, opening the door for the unrestrained sovereign. On this medium-sized planet of ours, these "affairs" can no longer be treated as "foreign," not by any definition.

We can never escape the central problem inherent in sovereign power, and must realize that our only option is to attempt to force oversight, *FLAWED LEADER)* accountability, and term limits on our power-holders. We may use laws and other such norms to refine our mechanisms for the limited delegation and the super-vision of executive power; we may build them into the fabric of our societies, even into the workings of our global community (through conventions, the body politic of the United Nations, and so on). Still, how-ever strong the institutions, the letter of the law will only describe the permissible limits of decision-mak-ing. Quite aside from the fact that law-fashioning is a slow process, even well-functioning laws cannot pre-scribe how to deal with every new situation, with every "case" of life as it unfolds, with every exception to the rule. That challenge remains, and it remains a very serious one.

The Camp as Sovereign Exception and the Fate of the Guantánamo Prisoners

Schmitt's terrible thesis, which holds such tremendous force for explaining the power of the pardon, has also been used by Giorgio Agamben as a starting point for a renewed investigation into the camp, that institutionalized practice of the ultimate suspension of normality in modern times. This is the "state of emergency" exemplified by its extreme, the industrial-style concentration camp, where normality and legality are suspended entirely—not just for birds or bears but for fellow human beings, and well beyond the confines of death row discussed above. This is, says Agamben, the "space that opens up when the state of exception starts to become the rule." Here, everything is generally and characteristically decided *case by case* outside any lawful process, instantly and without appeal, and with the total suspension of anything like a political citizenship.

The concentration camp can be regarded as the very *nomos* of the modern state, Agamben holds, because in it, the growth of formal rights of citizens increasingly and ominously correspond with a simultaneous inscription of their biological being into state procedures. In the camp, people are demoted from their former status as politically competent citizen-humans and radically reduced to a pure biopolitics—external political powers no longer confront citizens that have rights, but instead as "bare life." (See his *La comunitá che viene; Mezzi senza fine* and notably also

Homo sacer: Il potere sovrano e la nuda vita, in which Agamben aims to develop Foucault's biopolitical studies as the study of natural bodies in the modern body politic, and Hannah Arendt's on biopolitics and the camp.) Under this free reign of sovereign power, biopolitics becomes the only politics. The sovereign, notably, is altogether detached from the power of delegation and supervision that once remained with those ruled by him. How did this happen?

The story of the camp since the nineteenth century curiously shadows that of the industrialized states (not just Stalin's and Hitler's, but also the self-declared political democracies). From the camps set up by the Spanish in Cuba in the 1890s, to the British concentration camps in the Boer War in South Africa, to those of ubiquitous refugees—and on to its latest manifestation, the terror camp, the most famous of which is Guantánamo.

The denial of equal rights to the Guantánamo prisoners is but the tip of a large and threatening iceberg. Just to mention Europe, the tide of refugees is rising, and may already be creating the conditions in which people are herded into concentration camps, denuded and denied their right to equal treatment. Can the hope against hope held up by the Universal Declaration of Human Rights ensure every refugee's right to be treated as one-of-us, a fellow human and a fellow citizen? In the face of these questions Agamben has outlined the contours of a different, future *communitas* based no longer on an archaic, limited solidarity with the "we" of one's own against the "they" of the others. In my view, that hope will not be realized until humanity constructs global political organs that can constrain and supervise sovereign power—an inevitable fact of social life on this planet—and permit the exercise of such powers only under the ever-vigilant scrutiny of a global public.

Time is slipping away as the ongoing drama of the "outlaw" prisoners unfolds at the US-controlled camps at Guantánamo Bay, Cuba. The secretive spectacle is played out in the name of "security," and is off limits to true global public scrutiny, so that the phenomenon of "Guantánamo" by today is already infecting and poisoning the entire world. The prisoners, neither prisoners-of-war nor criminals, inhabit a zone opened up outside any law. Their status evokes the camp in that it exemplifies a state of exception, a tear in the fabric of the rule of law, a rift through which we can already see the sharp shadow of imperial sovereignty.

More than six hundred men have been held in the zone of exception opened up at the US prison camps at Guantánamo. Other such fighters are held elsewhere, in an equally secretive manner, in undisclosed locations around the world, without legal charges and without any recognized legal-political identity. They have been held captive as if their imprisonment was to be indefinite, waiting not even for a trial, sentence, or pardon, but simply for determination of their status and a timetable for the future. They were taken captive from the new global battlefield of the war on terror, dramatically expanded after the big bang of September 11, 2001—a "new war" with no end in sight. At first, they were held at a temporary "Camp X-Ray," then transferred to camps of preventive detention that are more permanent/indefinite. (The fact that both adjectives are appropriate is an illustration of what is now happening: A unilateral sovereign decision has been made to suspend the law and postpone indefinitely the definition of the status of the imprisoned.)

This has occurred despite numerous interventions from various states, organizations and individuals imploring the USA to respect and uphold the painstakingly constructed legal framework, norms, and principles for international coexistence, notably as expressed in the Geneva Convention on the Treatment on Prisoners of War. Another unilateral decision, to arrange for special military tribunals to try the captive "combatants," was announced, but has not been implemented. That decision has been equally harshly criticized and questioned.

Thus, the reconciliation of the sovereign action of extralegal imprisonment with international law has been indefinitely postponed—as if it will be unnecessary. Of course, to an unconstrained sovereignty it will not be. And the Guantánamo prisoners on Cuba are deliberately placed outside even the reach of the United States' own judicial system; the prisoners remain at the mercy of presidential decrees. In the absence of such decrees, there have been only singular pronouncements which serve to reinforce the indeterminacy of the situation. One example is the off-hand suggestion made by the US President early on, describing the captives as "killers," who would then, presumably, deserve to be put to death. Another example of this is the pronouncements made by lesser officials, suggesting instead the opposite, namely that many may be innocent and have been swept into Guantánamo unjustifiably.

It is astonishing that this arbitrary treatment also applies to persons who on paper are citizens of the US. Evidently, they too can now be detained and held captive *incommunicado* on the say-so of the executive branch of their government. Citizens have normally expected to be safe from secret detention by their own governments, at least not without clear and public judicial motivation and formal accusations under normal legal procedure. The exceptional, arbitrary state of the present situation is also evident in that several citizens of countries other than the US (France, Britain) have been detained and tried in regular courts for crimes of terrorism, while citizens of the US have been denied such treatment. These are all tell-tale signs that the very concept of citizenship is under reconstruction. Do they signal the start of a journey from citizenship to subjecthood? Many observers have pointed out that the kind of secretive treatment of citizens (of whatever country) that we have seen, even when carried out to prevent further horrendous terrorist attacks, will endanger the political rights enshrined in the basic tenets on which the US and similar rule-of-law states are supposedly founded.

Information about the Guantánamo prisoners is generally scarce. One day the news media report that they are well treated, the next that some have attempted suicide. Some reports say there are also juvenile prisoners. The Red Cross is allowed to visit, but on the usual condition that they reveal no information. American officials are quoted as saying the prisoners are treated "mostly" in accordance with the Geneva Convention, which is possible, but not proven. A handful of men were recently set free and unceremoniously sent back to Afghanistan. None of these repatriated men were accused of anything in a court of law and they apparently have received no redress.

One purported reason for the US shying away, so far, from clear submission to the Geneva Convention, is that if these men were defined as enemy soldiers in "war" and thus protected by the convention, their interrogation could not be pursued as it is now pursued (however that may be—we simply don't know). The same goes for those with US citizenship. But is this the main reason? Or is it also that the adversaries here are *intentionally* left undefined, or "vaguely" placed just beyond the grasp of definition?

Their captors have referred to the prisoners under many different names, including "terrorists." The latest label that seems to have stuck is "illegal enemy combatant"—an arbitrary category without basis in international law. (As commentators have pointed out, this phrase could be used for any "enemy" of the USA.) (Joseph Lelyveld's *New York Review of Books* article on Guantánamo on November 7, 2002 suggested the US military, who will continue to risk capture on future battlefields, are more interested in the issues of lawful reciprocity than are gov-

ernment executives, who will not have to face such
personal risk.)

Regarding the supposed indistinguishability of
the dual-faced enemies in Afghanistan—the international terrorist network and their pushed-about native
host regime, the fundamentalist Taliban—it has been
pointed out that while the Al Qaeda men may be
mercenaries of their own causes, the Taliban were
entitled to protection under the Convention. The
Taliban regime today is almost universally condemned, and rightly so. But we must note that it
originally was a functioning government, by any definition. The turn of events that drove the Taliban and
the terrorists into each other's arms must undoubtedly
be explained in part by the fact that the now-defunct
Taliban was hard pressed and heavily isolated by
severe international sanctions. In 2000, more sanctions were imposed through the UN by the big powers, over the obvious opposition of UN negotiators
who wished to continue talks with the Taliban.
Previously, the Taliban had even been able to declare
and observe an intention to protect non-Islamic culture in Afghanistan. Only after the sharpening of
sanctions and isolation did it reverse itself, under
increased pressure from its Al Qaeda benefactors, and
proceed with the bombing of the giant twin Bamiyan
Buddhas. That global-scale disaster in itself appears
to have been, above all, a media coup orchestrated by
Al Qaeda to attract attention to their goals. One clue
to understanding this may lie hidden in the little-
noticed report at the time which said that the Taliban
supreme commander, Mullah Omar, ordered a sacri-

fice of 100 head of cattle, twelve in Kabul and the
remainder around the rest of the severely drought-
stricken country. Their meat was to be distributed to
the poor. Officially, this was to atone for the delay in
the destruction of Bamiyan. Might it not have been,
instead, to atone for the shameful abandonment,
under the dictate of foreigners, of the Afghan sovereign prerogative? We may never know. But whatever
the complex relationship between the two faces of the
enemy, the continued US non-decision on the
Taliban/Al Qaeda status of these exceptional
Guantánamo prisoners would make sense as part of a
deliberate strategy of avoiding the prisoner-of-war
issue under international law and maintaining an
indeterminate enemy. As I write this, no one knows
what effects sporadic international protests against
this non-decision will have.

The captives are the citizens of forty or so
countries, including Afghanistan, and also one from
my own, Sweden. The Swede is 23 year-old Mehdi
Muhammed Ghezali who hails from the small town
of Örebro. In early February 2003, our government
began to ask for his release and said his treatment
disrespected international conventions. Surprisingly,
and ominously, Sweden was the first nation-in-wait-
ing to make such a demand among all the countries
whose citizens have been detained without charge or
trial. Next to nothing is known about what he may or
may not have done. There is a continuing local campaign on his behalf; his father once put himself in a
cage on one of Stockholm's public squares to highlight the case and continues to protest his son's

Figure 4. The father of the Swedish citizen imprisoned at Guantánamo making his case outside of the US embassy in Stockholm, Sweden, in 2002. By permission from Lena Hultén Sonne, Guantanamogruppen, Stockholm.

imprisonment without trial. (Fig. 4) (This tactic appears to have been adopted elsewhere in the world, as well, raising new questions about the meaning of citizenship.) Will this Swedish citizen be held indefinitely, will he be freed, or accused of some wrongdoing?

We are still waiting, and indeed, everyone seems to be growing accustomed to waiting indefinitely. In the meantime, it seems, a wholesale re-evaluation has begun of modern citizenship, international law, and notably also of the nation-states which among them were supposed to uphold that law. Perhaps the imagined international system of states was but a mirage. Some believe it has already been replaced by a new Rome that rules alone and by decree. Everything happens as if the actions of the most powerful are based on the principle that might is right—the very tendency that legal and political institutions in democracies were meant to circumscribe, temper, and overcome. To some this might also seem like a new version of the old saying: "becoming like your enemy." But this is about much more than one powerful state "going it alone" and adopting the tactics of the terrorists. It concerns a dangerous and infectious tendency to demolish and dispense with legality so as to give free reign to the unrestrained sovereign, and reduce would-be citizens into the means of imperial rule.

Imperial Sovereignty or Transparent Global Politics?

The turkey pardon and the story of Teddy's bear gave us prime examples of what the sovereign feeds on. He thrives on the decision of life-or-death. This is highlighted as merciful in the acts of public theater we have discussed, thereby elevating the sovereign in the eyes of the ruled, who become constituted as such subjects in this very moment of "shock and awe." Clearly, any argument that these are nothing but innocuous games falls to pieces on closer examination. It is not just that even the pardoned specimen is slaughtered, off camera, but that the rituals themselves represent, as we have seen, the sovereign's fundamental and structural antagonism towards normality, and therefore towards law and due political process. If there were no exceptions, the sovereign would not be needed. These childish games holding up the exceptional and the sovereign's merciful forgiveness fit the toying with life and death of the prisoner (and *toying* is the word). These are the exceptional decisions on which the sovereign thrives.

Looking closer at the radically indeterminate situation of the languishing Guantánamo prisoners, we cannot fail to notice precisely how their fate becomes dependent on singular, personal decisions made above international law, exceptional decisions. This is why Guantánamo entails such grave concern, beyond the individual fate of those humans being held there. By extension, the issue becomes whether or not this state of affairs can be reconciled with any kind of global political democracy.

We might turn pessimistic and think that the alternative future is more likely: a future in which one or several imperial sovereigns of the North dominate an increasingly apocalyptic, stateless South. The Northerners at the same time will endeavor to shield themselves from the chaos of this other world ravaged by open violence and by innumerable, uncontrollable small-arms wars (this is the scenario recently outlined in Herfried Münkler's book *Die neuen Kriege*). In such a world, competing sovereigns would invariably lend themselves to the resurrection of the old-time concept of the "barbarian" as the name of the enemy. We already hear its echoes in the state-sponsored understanding of the "terrorist." And in some distant future, the barbarian hordes might yet again overrun the empire.

Still in a pessimistic mode, we note that history teaches us that the barbarian is the imperial sovereign's favorite concept, the best friend who can be called to duty in many disguises. Barbarians typically serve as the violent, potentially dangerous not-us. As such, they have to be held at bay; at the same time, by virtue of their indispensability for the sovereign, they are always kept handy, ready to be invoked as the ultimate justification of his monopoly on the means and use of violence. In ancient China, the special bond between the "barbarian" and the emperor was expressed in a frighteningly beautiful formulation found in the philosophical classic, *Zhuangzi* ("Discourse on Swords" 10:30.3b). It describes the sword of the Son of Heaven as "wrapped in the Four Barbarians," one for each cardinal direction. The sharp edge of sovereign power, the personal control of the state monopoly on violence, is covered up and kept safe under the very threat of the barbarians, and thus always ready and waiting to be drawn and flashed out under this pretext. This archaic Chinese imperial concept of unbridled sovereignty built on the notion of the barbarian is timeless. Today it is re-emerging as a constant threat to any notion of equal world citizenship.

The "barbarian," pardoned or slaughtered at the sovereign's will, stands for what is naturally and by definition beyond the limit of the law, left in the hands of the sovereign. The barbarian is the human being towards whom one no longer needs to behave like a fellow human being. The concept of the barbarian and his inherent, threatening unpredictability is no vague concept, but a borderline concept (Schmitt, again) perfectly shaped to accompany the raw exercise of sovereign power. It will continue to serve as the justification for the emperor's keeping his sword long after the world has been conquered—and for his prerogative of acting on "foreign" affairs even in our midst, by opening new zones of emergency where legal protections for regular citizens are suspended.

But wait—is not the difference between the worlds of ancient Rome or China and our own the unstoppable advance of self (and other) awareness? Are we not part of a global community? This new interconnectedness is a foundation, one should like to hope, for institutions of global political scrutiny and oversight of any exercise of power, and for a possible global rule of law. And—why not—perhaps even for a global institution of pardon, which, of course, can serve much better ends than as the play-thing of the emperors of this world. It can be much more than the symbolic pardon of the poor turkey, blithely lingering on its pedestal in the President's garden, or the teddy bear, all too soon bathing in its own blood.

Yet, as pointed out by Sverker Åström, the Swedish senior diplomat, the USA twice recently—in the 1991 Gulf War and directly after September 11, 2001—passed up major, golden opportunities to rise above both extra-ordinary imperial manners and narrow patriotism to make a real difference for the world by embracing, reinforcing, and expanding the existing framework of rules to live by and for a global community, widely cherished and painstakingly constructed. Instead the issues of the day have been force-fit into the same old "Us" versus "Them."

The famous Paris newspaper *Le Monde* reached out on September 12, 2001, printing the defiant declaration that *Nous sommes tous des Américains* ("We are all Americans"). It was an appeal to the world for support for those hit by terror. Most people would want to join in such a call for solidarity. I do, too. Indeed, the vast majority of people on the planet do not want to see our hard-won rights and freedoms disrupted, curtailed or destroyed by totalitarians, fanatics, or any other threat. This is precisely why we should not fail to see, paraphrasing *Le Monde*, that we are all now prisoners of Guantánamo. ■

Acknowledgments

This text is based on research that has been ongoing since several years back, when I first noticed the strange turkey pardon ritual so faithfully carried out by every US President on the occasion of that most local of American feasts, Thanksgiving. The discovery was my own, but discoveries of this kind are generally made only when you know how to look for them. A great deal of credit for teaching me how to do that belongs with the late Valerio Valeri, Marshall Sahlins, Terence Turner, and the many other *aficionados* at the University of Chicago who take an interest in just what people do with, to, for, because of, or simply *thanks to* animals.

I published an article on the pardoning of the American Thanksgiving turkey in *Svenska Dagbladet*, one of the Stockholm dailies, on November 19, 2002, on the eve of the Thanksgiving of that year. A revised version of that article was later published in Turkish, as "Bag̈ıs̠lama ve Mutlak I˙ktidarın Gizi" (www.bianet.org/2003/04/18/18308.htm). I gratefully acknowledge permission to reuse some of the materials included in these previous texts. Yet another Stockholm daily, the *Aftonbladet*, kindly gave me credit for scattering the doubts shared by many in Sweden, that the turkey pardon ritual might have been nothing but a joke invented on the popular presidential TV show, *The West Wing*. What remained, however, was the misconceived idea that I was out to criticize the Americans or their country. I have no idea why my Swedish compatriots could have gotten that impression.

You may call my genre anthropology-at-home, if you wish, and if you are looking at the world strictly from the American point of view. But the piece is really written by an outsider looking in on the Thanksgiving table and the Rose Garden. To others it may simply be anthropology, period. But it really is an intentionally political kind of anthropology for our troubled times. I give many thanks to the publishers of the Prickly Paradigm Press for the honor of presenting this text as a prickly pamphlet, and to the editor, Matthew Engelke, for his diligent efforts.

Some Further Readings

• Turkeys, Thanksgivings, and such:

Loewen, James W. *Lies My Teacher Told Me. Everything Your American History Textbook Got Wrong.* New York: The New Press, 1995.

Murray, David. *Indian Giving. Economies of Power in Indian-White Exchanges.* Amherst: University of Massachusetts Press, 2000.

National Turkey Federation, *www.turkeyfed.org*

Schultz, Eric B. and Michael J. Tougias. *King Philip's War: The History and Legacy of America's Forgotten Conflict.* Woodstock, Vermont: Countryman Press, 2000.

The White House, Office of the Press Secretary, *www.whitehouse.gov/news/releases*

• Teddy bears and other animals:

Coetzee, J.M. *The Lives of Animals.* Princeton: Princeton University Press, 1999.

Hansen, Miriam. "Adventures of Goldilocks. Spectatorship, Consumerism and Public Life." *Camera Obscura* 22 (1990): 56-69.

Mullins, Linda. *The Teddy Bear Men. Theodore Roosevelt & Clifford Berryman.* 2nd edition. Grantsville, MD: Hobby House Press, 2002.

Roosevelt, Theodore. *American Bears. Selections from the Writings of Theodore Roosevelt.* Paul Schullery, ed. Boulder: Colorado Associated University Press, 1983.

• Moreover:

Agamben, Giorgio. *Homo Sacer: Sovereign Power and Bare Life.* Stanford: Stanford University Press, 1998.

Fiskesjö, Magnus. "On the 'Raw' and the 'Cooked' Barbarians of Imperial China." *Inner Asia* 1.2 (1999): 139-68.

Fleurdorge, Denis. *Les rituels du président de la République.* Paris: Presses Universitaires de France, 2001.

Kail, Michel et al, eds. *Les Temps Modernes.* Special issue, "La souveraineté: Horizons et figures de la politique." Vol. 55, No. 610, Sept.-Nov. 2000.

Kantorowics, Ernst H. *The King's Two Bodies. A Study in Medieval Political Theology.* Princeton: Princeton University Press, 1997.

Schmitt, Carl. *Political Theology: Four Chapters on the Concept of Sovereignty.* Cambridge: MIT Press, 1985.

Look for these titles by Prickly Paradigm, and others to come: